CULTURE
in India

Melanie Guile

Heinemann
LIBRARY

First published 2005 by Heinemann Library
a division of Harcourt Education Australia,
18–22 Salmon Street, Port Melbourne Victoria 3207 Australia
(a division of Reed International Books Australia Pty Ltd, ABN 70 001 002 357).
Visit the Heinemann Library website at www.heinemannlibrary.com.au

Published in Great Britain by Heinemann Library, Halley Court, Jordan Hill, Oxford OX2 8EJ,
part of Harcourt Education.
Visit the Heinemann Library UK website at www.heinemann.co.uk/library

A Reed Elsevier company

Commissioning: Carmel Heron
Editorial: Carmel Heron, Bronwyn Collie
Design: Stella Vassiliou, Marta White, Kerri Wilson
Photo research: Legend Images, Wendy Duncan
Production: Tracey Jarrett
Map: Guy Holt

Typeset in Bembo 12.5pt
Film separations by Digital Imaging Group (DIG), Melbourne
Printed in China by WKT Company Ltd.

The paper used to print this book comes from sustainable resources.

National Library of Australia Cataloguing-in-Publication data:
Guile, Melanie, 1949– .
    Culture in India.
    Includes index.

    For primary and secondary students.
    ISBN 1 74070 179 8.

    1. India – Civilization – Juvenile literature. 2. India –
    Social life and customs – Juvenile literature. I. Title.
    (Series : Guile, Melanie, 1949– Culture in...)

954

Acknowledgements
The publisher would like to thank the following for permission to reproduce photographs: AFP Photo:
pp. 11, 23 (lower), 25, 28; Australian Picture Library/Corbis: pp. 13, 23 (upper), /Corbis/Michael Boys:
p. 17; Dinodia Photo Library: pp. 8, 9, 10 (both), 19, 20, 21, 24, 26, 29; Getty Images/Aris Messinis/AFP:
p. 18, /Robert Nickelsberg/Time Life Pictures: p. 15 (upper), /Prakash Singh/AFP: p. 15 (lower); Lonely
Planet Images/Richard I'Anson: p. 27, /Liz Thompson: p. 12, /Eric Wheater: p. 7; Photolibrary.com: p. 16,
/Index Stock: p. 14.

Cover photograph of Great Elephant Show reproduced with permission of Australian Picture
Library/Corbis/Blaine Harrington III.

Every attempt has been made to trace and acknowledge copyright. Where an attempt has been
unsuccessful, the publisher would be pleased to hear from the copyright owner so any omission or error can
be rectified.

CONTENTS

Culture in India   4

Traditions and customs   8

Minority groups   12

Costume and clothing   14

Food   16

Performing arts   18

Literature   22

Film and television   24

Arts and crafts   26

Glossary   30

Index   32

Words that appear in bold,
like this, are explained in the
glossary on pages 30 and 31.

CULTURE IN *India*

The great wedge of India hangs from the Asian continent between the Arabian Sea in the west and the Bay of Bengal in the east. Its position at the crossroads between Europe and Asia meant that waves of invaders swept through the country over thousands of years. They added their cultures to those of the **indigenous** tribal peoples, many of whom still survive in remote areas. All these different **ethnic groups** have left India with one of the world's richest cultures, dating back more than 5000 years.

What is culture?

Culture is a people's way of living. It is the way in which people identify themselves as a group, separate and different from any other. Culture includes a group's spoken and written language, social customs and habits, as well as its traditions of art, craft, dance, drama, music, literature and religion.

India's **diversity** of religions, languages and cultures mean there are thousands of little Indias flourishing within one nation. Government attempts to encourage a national focus have only partly succeeded, and in elections people still vote along **caste** and religious lines. Nevertheless, there are many shared values.

Throughout India, the family is the centre of people's lives, with several generations living together in extended families, and men making the important decisions. Many families arrange important celebrations after consulting an astrological chart (*kundali*) to find the luckiest date.

The great national religion, **Hinduism**, binds the majority together with common goals, duties and rituals. Tolerance is also an important shared value in this **multicultural** country of more than a billion people.

Languages

More than 1500 languages are spoken in India, and 18 are officially recognised. Hindi is spoken by 20 per cent of the population and is the language of government. Other main languages are Bengali, Gujarati, Urdu, Punjabi, Tamil and English. Hindi shares many similarities with **Sanskrit**, the ancient language of classical Indian literature.

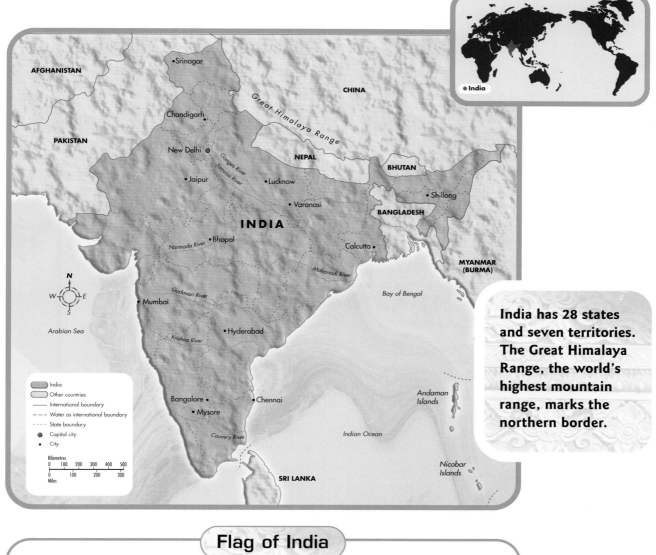

India has 28 states and seven territories. The Great Himalaya Range, the world's highest mountain range, marks the northern border.

Flag of India

The national flag of India is called the *tiranga* (three colours). The saffron (orange) stands for courage, the white for purity and peace, and the green for faith and **fertility**. The symbol in the centre is the ancient chakra (wheel of law).

Land of extremes

India is a land of contrasts and extremes. Massive industrial growth and success in technology has brought great wealth to the top third of the population. The growing middle class lives in reasonable conditions, but 233 million people still have no education or health care, and go to bed hungry every night. Although school is **compulsory** to age 14, only about 60 per cent of children attend, and only about 60 per cent of the population can read and write.

History

Around 2500 BC the people of the **Indus Valley** created great cities, pottery and artworks in what is now Pakistan. Lighter-skinned people called Aryans from central Asia overran this **civilisation** around 1500 BC. They introduced the **Hindu** religion and its **caste system**, which divides people into classes. They also drove India's original inhabitants, the Dravidians, into the south.

The great Mauryan empire arose around 300 BC, with Ashoka as its most famous emperor. He encouraged a new religion called **Buddhism**, which began in Nepal around 500 BC. Around AD 1000, **Muslims** from the Middle East overran the north, where their religion still flourishes. The **Mughals** invaded in 1526 and later built magnificent monuments, including the famous Taj Mahal in Agra. The British ruled India from the 1800s until independence in 1947. They left behind English education and legal systems, and the game of cricket – India's most popular sport.

Partition

At the time of independence, Muslim areas in the north were **partitioned** off from India to form the new countries of Pakistan in the west and Bangladesh in the east. Although the aim was to reduce religious tension between Muslims and Hindus, disputes over borders and religious issues have often resulted in war between India and Pakistan.

Gandhi – man of peace

One of the world's great leaders, Mohandas Karamchand (Mahatma) Gandhi (1869–1948), is best known for his idea of nonviolent protest. Born into a wealthy family, he championed the rights of the poor, particularly the Dalits (untouchables). He fought for Indian independence from Britain through nonviolent protests such as hunger strikes and workers' strikes. Named Mahatma (Great Soul), Gandhi was greatly loved, and all India mourned when he was **assassinated** in 1948.

The people

India has the world's second-largest population, with almost 1.05 billion people and 5653 different **ethnic groups**. Around 72 per cent of people live in the country on farms. Hundreds of **indigenous** tribes live in remote communities outside the main culture. The average **life expectancy** is only 63 years. India is a **democracy** and its prime minister is Shri Atal Bihari Vajpayee.

Religions

Around 83 per cent of Indians are Hindus. They worship hundreds of gods and goddesses, each a form of the supreme being, Brahman. Hindus believe in **reincarnation**, or being reborn as something either better or worse, depending on your deeds (*karma*). Lower castes and Dalits (untouchables) cannot achieve *moksha* (freedom from rebirth). Doing your duty (*dharma*), studying the holy texts (the Vedas), making temple offerings, becoming a holy man (*sadhu*) and bathing in the sacred River Ganges are ways of improving your chances of achieving *moksha*.

Muslims make up 12 per cent of the population and live mainly in the north. Although there has often been tension between Muslims and Hindus, for the most part they live together peacefully. Other religious groups include **Sikhs**, **Christians** and **Jains**. The Himalayan states of the far north are mostly Buddhist.

TRADITIONS
and customs

With such a rich culture, Indians have learned to live with contrasts. **Sacred** cows that, according to **Hindu** custom, must be allowed to roam free, graze on the edge of six-lane freeways. Farmers plough with bullocks beside leading-edge technology factories.

Mosques, temples, gurudwaras and churches exist side by side. Top women executives still wear the red *bindi* (spot on the forehead), which stands for *shakti* (female energy). Great leaders like Gandhi and Jawaharlal (Pandit) Nehru, independent India's first prime minister, united the people in peaceful nationhood. Indians are proud of belonging to the world's largest **democracy**. Nevertheless, deep divisions persist.

India is a place of extremes, with old and new existing side by side.

The caste system

All Hindus are born into a **caste** that dictates where they live, who they can marry and what jobs they can do. Castes are ranked from Brahmins (traditionally priests) at the top, through Kshatriyas (warriors), Vaishyas (merchants) and Shudras (servants or labourers) at the bottom. The top three castes (the 'twice-born') are permitted to read the sacred Hindu texts (Vedas), but Shudras are not. Below these ranks are the 'untouchables' (now called Dalits, meaning 'broken ones'). People cannot change their caste and often must marry within it. Although laws have been passed to outlaw the caste system, most believe they have been ineffective.

In spite of laws to protect them, Dalits still suffer **discrimination**.

Great Dalit leader

Dr Bhimrao Ramji Ambedkar, born a Dalit, became a lawyer and fought for justice and equality for all castes. He rose to become the minister for law and single-handedly drafted the Indian **constitution**, which guarantees Dalits seats in parliament, university places and government jobs.

Dalits

Dalits make up 20 per cent of the population. Labelled as polluted in ancient Hindu texts, they were denied education and restricted to the dirtiest jobs. Higher-caste Hindus would not touch or mix with them. Untouchability was banned in 1950, and laws were passed to favour Dalits, but most still own no land, at least 50 per cent live in poverty, only around 40 per cent can read and write, and their average life expectancy, at 42 years, is more than 20 years lower than that of other Indians.

Women and girls

Women usually come second to men in Indian society. They are often expected to obey and serve their husbands and sons, and work many more hours than men. Girls are regarded as burdens because huge **dowries** must be paid by their families when they marry. Male babies are celebrated because they will later take care of the family. Although these attitudes are officially discouraged, and educated men and women speak out against them, many women terminate (stop) their pregnancies if they know they are carrying a girl. This has led to more boys than girls being born, at 100 males to every 93 females.

On the positive side, since 1993 one-third of local government seats have been set aside for women, which has greatly increased their involvement in politics. In 1966, India elected one of the world's first female prime ministers, Indira Gandhi.

Hindu marriage

Most **Hindu** marriages are arranged by the parents of the intended couple, although the young woman can refuse the match. The couple must have the same star sign according to the *janam kundali* (horoscope), and a **dowry** may

be set. At an engagement ceremony, the groom's family gives the bride a wedding *sari*. The wedding itself is held under a canopy, where the couple have their feet washed, join hands and exchange flower wreaths. They then walk around a **sacred** fire seven times chanting prayers in a ritual called the *saptapadi*. Guests throw rice and petals for wealth and happiness.

Hindu marriage ceremonies include numerous **rituals**. The traditional red *sari* is worn to bring good luck.

Religious festivals

With so many different cultural groups, festivals fill the calendar. **Buddhists** in the Himalayan states of Sikkim and Himachal Pradesh celebrate *Buddha Jayanti* (in May or June), or the birth and **enlightenment** of Lord Buddha. **Christians** fill the churches during Christmas and Easter. Individual Hindu gods and goddesses have their own special days, like the *Ganesh Chaturthi* festival (in August or September) in honour of the popular elephant-headed god of luck and success, Ganesh.

At *Ganesh Chaturthi*, Hindus pray to the god Ganesh for good luck and happiness.

People spray each other with coloured water during *Holi*.

Festival of Lights

Deepavali or *Divali,* the Festival of Lights (October or November), is the most important Hindu festival. Families clean their houses, buy new clothes and gather to celebrate the New Year. Little clay lamps (*diyas*) are lit to welcome the goddess of wealth, Lakshmi, into the home, and fairy lights are hung in city streets. Special sticky sweets called *halva* and *coconut burfi* are eaten, and gifts are exchanged.

Holi

Holi (February or March) is a spring festival to worship Lord Krishna. The night before, Hindus make temple offerings during the *puja* ritual, and afterwards light a huge bonfire. But most people enjoy the fun part of *Holi*. This involves throwing coloured water or coloured powder called *gulal* over everyone in sight. Many end up covered with different colours and soaking wet. At noon the fun stops, and people go home to wash and change.

Id-ul-Fitr

Id-ul-Fitr means 'feast of the breaking of the fast', and is the most important festival for **Muslims**. It marks the end of the 30-day fasting period of Ramzan (Ramadan), in the ninth month of the Muslim calendar, during which Muslims do not eat or drink from sunrise to sunset. Families attend mosque early, dressed in new clothes, and give money and food to charity. Afterwards there is lots of eating and visiting with family and friends.

Toda rituals

The **indigenous** Toda people worship nature and the buffalo. They celebrate a baby's birth by presenting it to the sacred buffalo at a 'naming ceremony'. The baby's head is shaved and its face is uncovered for the first time. It is then displayed to the dairy herd. Female babies are fed buttermilk. Male babies have their heads touched at the dairy door.

MINORITY GROUPS

With around 635 different tribes, India has the world's largest number of **indigenous** people (called *adivasis* or Scheduled Tribes). *Adivasis* make up around eight per cent of the population, and include the ancient bowmen, the Bhils; the tribal Santhals; the Toda of Tamil Nadu; and the coastal Halakkis.

A young Bhil groom before his wedding ceremony.

Below even the Dalits in the **Hindu caste system**, *adivasis* are India's most disadvantaged people. In spite of many laws to help them, **discrimination**, a lack of educational opportunities and the loss of land threaten their ways of life.

The Santhals and the Bhils

The Santhals are India's largest tribal group, numbering around 10 million. Concentrated in the eastern and central states, they were originally forest-dwelling farmers, but in the 1900s many **migrated** to work in the tea plantations of Assam and West Bengal. Today, most Santhals work in quarrying and labouring jobs, and are among the poorest people in the country.

Around one million Bhils live in central India. Originally hunters with a warlike reputation, today they live in small farming communities under a headman called the *tadvi*. Most Bhil are Hindu, but some also worship stone images and the spirits of the forest. Traditional Bhil weddings are very costly and include up to 50 separate **rituals**. In one, animal and human figures are drawn on the walls of the bridal hut, and the couple walks seven times anticlockwise around a **sacred** pole.

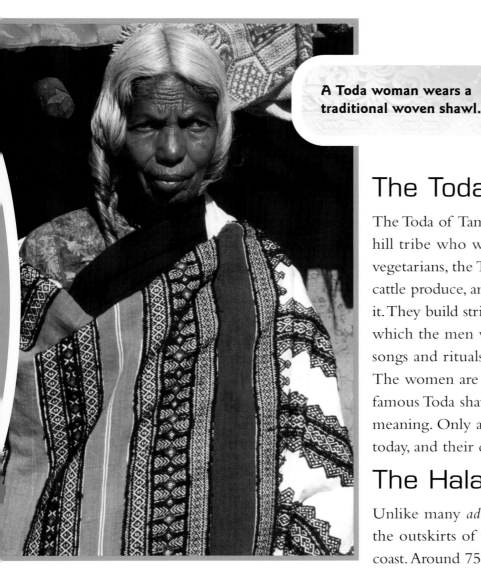

A Toda woman wears a traditional woven shawl.

The Toda

The Toda of Tamil Nadu are an ancient forest hill tribe who worship the buffalo. Strict vegetarians, the Toda live off the milk their cattle produce, and the butter they make from it. They build striking, cone-shaped shrines in which the men worship, and have important songs and rituals based on the buffalo. The women are skilled at embroidering the famous Toda shawls, which have sacred meaning. Only around 1000 Toda survive today, and their culture is fast disappearing.

The Halakki farmers

Unlike many *adivasis*, the Halakkis live on the outskirts of towns on the south-west coast. Around 75 000 Halakkis live in thatched mud huts decorated with abstract wall paintings known as *hali*. The women (*gowdathis*) are famous for the masses of necklaces, bangles and other jewellery they wear. During the *Holi* festival, the men perform a harvest dance (*suggi kunita*) wearing spectacular costumes. These include a red and yellow *kurta pyjama* and a lavish headpiece (*turayi*) made of flowers, beads and paper. The men also carry a bunch of peacock feathers (*kuncha*) and drumsticks (*kolu*) as they dance in a circle to singing and the beat of drums.

Ghotuls – forest schools

Tribal people all over central India have an education system that dates back thousands of years. Jungle schools called *ghotuls* are run by the young people. All aspects of tribal living are taught, including leaf weaving, wood carving, singing and dancing. Married people are not allowed into the schools, and young children learn from older ones.

COSTUME
and clothing

According to ancient Indian beliefs, unstitched cloth is more pure, so many Indian costumes are simply lengths of material wrapped around the head or body. Their beauty comes from the brilliant colours, the different weaves and the decorations on the fabrics, many of which are still hand-woven and embroidered by village people.

Traditional clothing

Women everywhere wear traditional clothes, and fashion designers bring out new versions each year.

The national dress of Indian women is the *sari*. It is made of a 6-metre length of material, usually with an embroidered or woven border. It is worn with a short, tight blouse and a long draw-string petticoat. *Saris* are wrapped to form a graceful, long dress with the tail (the decorated *pallu*) draped over the shoulder, leaving the midriff bare.

The *salwar kameez* is worn all over northern India. A flowing tunic dress (*kameez*) is worn over loose trousers drawn tight at the ankles. A light scarf (*dupatta*) is draped around the neck and often covers the head.

Traditional men's clothing is simple: a piece of cloth wrapped around the waist (a *lungi*), or a length of material wrapped around the hips and between the legs to form trousers (*dhoti*). The *kurta pyjama* consists of a long shirt and loose white trousers. However, apart from farm labourers, few Indian men wear traditional clothing today, preferring western-style shirts and trousers.

The graceful *sari* is the oldest recorded traditional costume in the world.

The language of gold

Indian women wear their wealth in the form of jewellery. Gold was thought to purify the skin, and is still very popular. Bangles are believed to protect the wearer, and a nose stud is a symbol of purity. A special necklace called a *mangalasutra* is worn as a wedding token, and toe and ankle rings are worn mainly by married women.

The *pheta* is a huge turban made of 6 metres of cloth.

Sikh men wear turbans, consisting of a long piece of plain material wrapped tightly around the head. In Rajasthan and Maharashtra, men wear a *pheta* – 6 metres of cloth wound in **intricate** folds to form a huge turban.

Folk costumes

Brilliant colours and gleaming mirror-work embroidery are favoured by the women of Rajasthan and Gujarat. They wear a long, pleated skirt called a *ghaghra* or *lehenga*, teamed with a backless blouse (*choli*), both elaborately embroidered, and a cotton scarf (*dupatta*). Chunky bangles, earrings and anklets complete the *ghaghra choli* outfit.

Indian fashion industry

Indian designers are famous for their luxurious fabrics and glamorous styles. Leading designer Rohit Bal was named 'India's master of fabric and fantasy' by America's *Time* magazine. His 2003 collection featured embroidered men's jackets and traditional *lungi* with zips and leather belts!

Even better known is Ritu Kumar, who brought traditional, handmade fabrics to high fashion. Among her famous clients was the late Princess Diana. Kumar also makes the gowns for Miss India in beauty pageants.

Gowns by Ritu Kumar are in demand around the world.

FOOD

India is the home of hot, spicy food, much of which is vegetarian. Dozens of different spices are used in cooking, including chilli, cloves, coriander, cumin, cardamom and turmeric. These are freshly ground and fried to bring out the rich flavours, then cooked with vegetables, lamb, fish or chicken to make spicy stews. Rice accompanies almost every meal, and is the staple or basic food in southern India. In the north, wheat flour breads are eaten as well.

Originally from the south, *thali* is now eaten throughout India.

South Indian food

Most meals in the south are rice-based. A very common dish is *thali*, which is often served on a large banana leaf. It consists of a mound of boiled white rice with curried vegetables, plus small side dishes of yogurt, chutney, pickles and sometimes a tasty **lentil** stew called *dhal*. Small snacks are usually eaten for breakfast. These include *idli*, which are rice and lentil cakes steamed and served with a thick tomato and lentil sauce (*sambar*) and coconut chutney. *Pongal*, a dish of spiced sticky rice, is also a popular breakfast meal.

Food in the north

More meat is eaten in northern India, reflecting the influence of the **Mughals** who occupied the area for around 200 years (1526–1707). They introduced the *tandoor*, a clay oven for slow cooking to bring out subtle flavours. Tandoori chicken is soaked in herbs and yogurt before cooking, and is famously tender. *Biryani* consists of meat mixed with spicy rice and dried fruits. *Kebabs* (meat threaded on to skewers and grilled) are also popular in the north. Lamb, chicken and fish are eaten, but pork is forbidden to **Muslims**, and **Hindus** do not eat beef because the cow is **sacred** to them.

Wheat is grown in the colder north, so wheat-flour bread is baked there, either in the *tandoor* (*naan*) or on a hot plate (*roti* or *chapati*). *Parathas* are breads cooked in butter and often stuffed with curried potatoes and vegetables. Puffed-up, crisp *pappadams* are deep-fried lentil flour wafers and are popular around the world.

Street vendors offer a huge variety of snacks, called *tiffin*, which are eaten on the run.

Finger food

People throughout India eat with their fingers, but there is a knack to it. Only the right hand is used (the left is considered unclean). Food is scooped into little mounds and carried up to the mouth with the four fingers, then the thumb shovels the morsel into the mouth. Only the thumb touches the lips, leaving the other fingers clean to return to the plate. It is considered impolite to dirty your fingers beyond the second joint.

Meals on wheels

Office workers in the city of Mumbai do not have to put up with boring cold lunches. Many wives cook three-course hot meals and put them in lunch boxes called *dabbas*. Delivery men called *dabbawallahs* pick them up and deliver them to the offices, and return the containers afterwards. Although most *dabbawallahs* cannot read, markings on the *dabbas* help them distinguish between the boxes. *Dabbawallahs* are found only in Mumbai. The trade is dying out due to the increasing number of working women and the fact that many businesspeople do not have time to eat elaborate midday meals.

PERFORMING ARTS

In India, music, dance and drama began as a form of Hindu temple worship. The basics of the classical style were written down by Bharata Muni around 2000 years ago, in a book called the *Natya Shastra*. This text has shaped traditional Indian music ever since.

Traditional music

Indian classical music uses quarter-tones and sliding scales to create a flowing, multi-layered sound. There are two main types – Hindustani from northern India and Carnatic from the south – but they share many common features. Usually the rhythm (*tala*) is beaten out by a drum, the background 'drone' or hum comes from base instruments, and a singer or main instrument creates the *raga* or melody. Singers are highly skilled and **improvise** around the *ragas*, which convey different moods.

Instruments

Traditional stringed instruments can be played with a bow, but most are plucked. The *sitar* is a long-necked, guitar-like instrument usually with 17 strings plus 'sympathetic strings' inside the neck that vibrate to give a magical, echoing sound. The ancient *veena*, from southern India, is like a large mandolin with a ball-shaped echo chamber attached to the neck.

Sitar **master Ravi Shankar introduced this classical instrument to the west when he taught George Harrison of The Beatles to play it in the 1960s.**

Twin drums called *tabla* commonly set the beat. On the skins is a black spot made of gum, soot and iron filings, which makes a bell-like sound when struck. Clappers, cymbals and large drums are also used. Bamboo flutes called *bansuri* are popular. The flute used by snake charmers is called a *pungi*. It consists of two tubes attached to a hollowed-out coconut that contains **vibrating** reeds. It makes an eerie sound when blown. Traditional orchestras generally consist of five or six players and accompany classical singers.

Modern sounds

Bhangra is a modern fusion of Indian folk music with rap, reggae and rhythm and blues. Based on Punjabi folk music with its wild drum rhythms, it is huge in dance clubs in the UK and Asia. Punjabi singer-songwriter Daler Mehndi is known in India as 'the king of *bhangra*'. He used modern western instruments and lyrics along with *bhangra* folk traditions in his 1995 smash hit album, *Bolo Ta Ra Ra*. Daler Mehndi's up-beat songs and rich voice, along with his jewelled turban, have won him international fame.

Indipop

Around 70 per cent of albums sold in India are songs from films made in the city of Mumbai (often called Bollywood). Soundtracks blend Indian classical music with a folksy flavour, and singers have huge followings.

But Indian pop music was unknown until singer Alisha Chinai released her *Made in India* album in 1994. She mixed western pop sounds with traditional Indian music to create Indipop, which took the country by storm. Today, Indipop is extremely popular. There is even a 'manufactured' all-girl band called Viva, whose members were hand-picked by a national TV station.

Classical drama

Dance, music and storytelling come together in the ancient dance-drama known as the *kutiyattam*. Originally performed only in temples, the drama begins with an actor (*chakyar*) addressing the audience in the ancient **Sanskrit** language. Characters wear make-up and elaborate costumes and use mime, voice and a group of drummers to tell religious stories.

Classical dance

Kathak, from northern India, is a blend of ancient dance-drama and **Muslim** influences. The performers use mime and dance to relate **Hindu epic** tales. The dance includes rapid spins and foot-stamping, and dancers wear ankle bells that jingle as they move. Traditionally *kathak* was danced by women, accompanied by traditional instruments.

The *bharata natyam* comes from the southern state of Tamil Nadu and is one of the oldest dances in India. Female dancers called *devadasis* traditionally lived in Hindu temples, and handed down their skills to their daughters. Graceful movements and facial expressions convey emotions in this carefully controlled dance of jumps, spins and balanced poses.

Very different in mood is the energetic men's dance called the *kathakali*, which comes from Kerala in southern India. The men wear green face make-up, large gold headdresses and swinging robes as they perform spectacular, all-night dances in the open air, accompanied by a traditional orchestra of *tabla*, strings and flute.

The classical solo dance, *bharata natyam*, from southern India, uses hand gestures (*mudras*) and facial expressions to convey emotions.

PERFORMING ARTS

Men perform the *bhangra* dance at a festival in Punjab.

Folk dance

Apart from classical dances, smaller communities of people also had folk dances to celebrate important events. The *chhau* from Orissa began as a martial art. Masked dancers leap and spin, often using swords or shields with great skill. In the Punjab, the *bhangra* developed as a harvest festival dance. Lively movements are accompanied by singing and the rapid beat of the *dhol* drum and *chimta* (metal clappers). The *bhangra* gave its name to a popular form of modern music based on the raw energy of the dance.

Puppet theatre

Puppet theatre was invented in India more than 1000 years ago. All puppet forms are found there, including stringed **marionettes**, rod puppets and glove puppets. Flat leather 'shadow puppets' are worked by rods and strings from behind a lit screen. The life-sized figures are made of dyed and **intricately** carved goat skin, and glow with colour when the light shines through them.

LITERATURE

Literature has been an important part of India's culture for thousands of years, and some of the world's oldest works were written there. Today's internationally successful writers continue the tradition.

Ancient literature

The great **Hindu** holy books, the Vedas, were written around 1500–1200 BC. The first book, the Rig Veda, has 1028 verses of creation stories and prayers, and is written in the ancient **Sanskrit** language. The Vedas are regarded as the word of god and form the basis of the Hindu religion.

Hindu epic tales

Begun around 1000 BC, the *Mahabharata* is a collection of stories, including descriptions of the heroic deeds of the Hindu god Krishna and his battles against evil demons. It is the world's largest work of literature.

Even better known is the *Ramayana*. It was written around 300 BC by Valmiki, a robber turned singer-poet. Written in Sanskrit verse, the *Ramayana* tells of the god Rama's love for the beautiful Sita, and how he saved her from the villain Ravana with the help of Hanuman, the mischievous monkey-god. Today, tales from the *Ramayana* are retold in traditional drama and puppet performances, and a 78-part television series based on it brought all India to a stop every Sunday during 1987 and 1988.

Sanskrit master

India's greatest Sanskrit writer, Kalidasa, lived around AD 350–400. He wrote only three plays and four poems, but is greatly admired for his realistic characters and the beauty of his language. His masterpiece is a poem of 111 verses titled *Meghaduuta*. It describes a man who, separated from his wife, writes of the sad beauty of the landscape and his feelings of loss.

Man of Malgudi

R K Narayan (1906–2001) is India's best-loved writer in English. He created the imaginary town, Malgudi, which became the setting for many stories, including the famous *Malgudi Days* and *Under the Banyan Tree*. His charming descriptions of ordinary people and everyday life won him many awards around the world.

World poet

Legendary writer Rabindranath Tagore (1861–1941) was born in Calcutta, and wrote plays, stories and poetry. His book of poems, *Geetanjali*, caused a sensation in London, and in 1913 he won the Nobel Prize for Literature. Tagore was also a painter, teacher and musician, and wrote the Indian national anthem, '*Jana Gana Mana*' ('Thou Art the Ruler of All Minds').

The poet Rabindranath Tagore in 1929.

Arundhati Roy won the Booker Prize for her novel *The God of Small Things*.

Literature today

India has produced a host of internationally renowned writers. Vikram Seth received high praise for his novel, *A Suitable Boy* (1993), a family saga full of lively and unusual characters. Arundhati Roy wrote the novel *The God of Small Things*, for which she won the Booker Prize in 1997. It explores the evils of the **caste system** through the lives of two children.

Ruth Prawer Jhabvala was born in Germany into a Jewish family but lived in India for many years. She wrote nine novels, including the Booker Prize-winning *Heat and Dust*. She has also won two Academy Awards for her film scripts (*A Room with a View* in 1985 and *Howards End* in 1992).

Anita Desai is famous for her novels, including *Fire on the Mountain* (1977), and the award-winning children's book, *The Village by the Sea* (1982). Her daughter, Kiran Desai, wrote the international best-seller *Hullabaloo in the Guava Orchard* (1998).

FILM
and television

India has the world's largest film industry, with audiences in the hundreds of millions and big-budget studios. Television is also extremely popular, and locally produced programs are generally preferred to imported ones.

Film pioneers

In 1913, Dadasaheb Phalke (1870–1944) screened his first movie, *Raja Harishchandra*, based on an Indian **epic** tale. His studio near Bombay made around 95 silent movies before 'talkies' put him out of business. The first sound film screened in India was *Alam Ara* (1931), by director Ardershir Irani. It featured seven songs, and musical numbers have been a part of Indian blockbuster movies ever since.

Golden era of film

The 1950s saw the rise of filmmaker Satyajit Ray, who is regarded as one of the world's great directors. Ray created realistic, moving stories about ordinary people. His famous first film, *Pather Panchali* (*Song of the Road*, 1955), about a poor village boy named Apu, is now a classic. Ray was awarded an Oscar for Lifetime Achievement on his deathbed in 1992.

Bollywood

Lavish costumes and sets, unlikely plots and glamorous stars are all found in the popular movies made in the Mumbai (previously Bombay) studios known as **Bollywood**. Called 'masala movies' because they include a bit of everything (like masala spice mix), the films combine fantasy, singing, dancing, violence and romance.

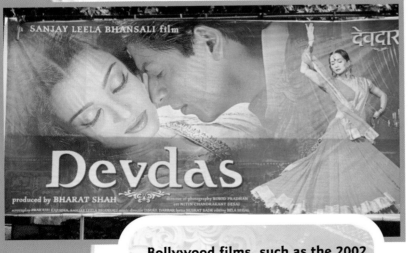

Bollywood films, such as the 2002 hit *Devdas*, are advertised with striking posters.

Singing superstar

He was short, plain and balding, but Kundan Lal Saigal (1904–1947) was India's first film star. Acting during the 1930s and 1940s, his brilliant voice and brooding looks suited tragic hero roles in which he sang, danced and wore a wig to hide his thinning hair!

Bollywood star Madhuri Dixit hosts the popular reality television show *Kahin naa Kahin koi hai*.

Star attractions

Shah Rukh (S R) Khan is one of India's top movie stars. He made his debut in 1988 in the TV hit series, *Fauji*, a soap about a group of military trainees. Although critics pan his over-dramatic style, movie-goers love him. He starred in the Bollywood remake of the tragic love epic *Devdas* in 2002, the most expensive Indian film ever made. His co-star was former Miss World, Aishwarya Rai, India's hottest Bollywood actress.

International successes

Bombay-born producer-director Ismail Merchant, with American partner James Ivory, has won high praise for his fine **adaptations** of English classic novels. Actor turned writer-director Mira Nair's sensitive first feature, *Salaam Bombay!* (1988), won 26 awards and is regarded as a classic. Her 2000 feature, *Monsoon Wedding*, was also an international success. London-raised Gurinder Chadha achieved a hit with her cross-cultural movie, *Bend It Like Beckham* (2002), about a **Sikh** girl in England who wants to play soccer.

Television

Around 80 per cent of people in India have a television. The government owns and controls some stations, and private satellite TV is growing. Local versions of American dramas, sitcoms and game shows are popular. The top soap is *Kyunki Saas Bhi Kabhi Bahu Thi*, a Cinderella-style comedy-drama about three nasty aunts-in-law and their long-suffering *bahu* (daughter/niece-in-law), Tulsi. Reality TV became popular in 2002 with *Kahin naa Kahin koi hai* (*There is someone out there*), a show that arranges marriages on the spot for young singles. It is hosted by top film actress, Madhuri Dixit.

ARTS AND CRAFTS

Pottery statues found in the **Indus Valley** (in modern-day Pakistan) show that uniquely Indian art styles existed 5000 years ago. Over the centuries, the skills of artists and artisans were refined, and today modern masters create a huge variety of arts and crafts.

The Ajanta cave paintings

For 800 years, from around 200 BC, the monks at Ajanta painted scenes from the lives of the **Buddha** on the walls of their monastery caves. Today, the Ajanta cave paintings are world famous for the beauty and detail of the figures. The rock walls were first coated with hair and clay plaster, then painted with natural dyes, and finally polished to a sheen with stone. To this day, artists regard the Ajanta paintings as the best in Indian art, and many modern works are based on them.

Buddhist monks created the World-Heritage-listed Ajanta cave paintings over a period of 800 years.

Stone masterpieces

The great Buddhist emperor Ashoka (around 300 BC) encouraged the arts, and ordered great monuments to be built. One is the famous **Stupa** of Sanchi, in Madhya Pradesh. Built from stone-covered brick, the stupa marks a sacred place for Buddhists, but is best known for the huge stone pillar topped with a carving of four lions. This ancient design was chosen as the emblem of the new India at independence in 1947. Four huge stone gateways (*toranas*) were added in the first century BC to represent the four corners of the universe. Made by ivory carvers, the gates are covered with finely detailed animals and human figures, including elephants, monkeys and scenes from the life of the Buddha.

Folk art

For centuries, Indian women have decorated the walls of their houses with patterns or pictures. In the state of Bihar, animals, goddesses and scenes of village life were painted in bold, simple designs. Known as *mithila* paintings, they were originally done to bless the marriage chamber. Women used household spices as colours and applied them with bamboo twigs. Since the 1960s, the strong, simple designs have been created on paper and sold to collectors.

Kalighat paintings (*pats*) were originally made as souvenirs for holy pilgrims to the Kali Temple in Calcutta. They were simple watercolour sketches of Hindu gods done by **anonymous** artists (called *patua*) to earn extra money. Subjects were often humorous, and were depicted in bold colours and lively styles. *Pats* were created from around 1830 to 1930, after which printed images took over, but they are highly regarded by collectors today.

Framed prints of Hindu gods are displayed for sale at a market stall outside the Kali Temple.

The Black Pagoda

The Sun Temple of Konarak was built around AD 1250 from black sandstone. Its tall roof is covered with sculptures of female musicians welcoming the sun god as he travels across the sky. Aruna, the Lord of Dawn, is shown driving his huge chariot, led by seven stone horses. A large sculpture of the god Surya is carved out of green stone, in glowing contrast to the black temple.

The birth of modern art

By the 1900s, Indian artists were looking for new ways to express themselves. In Calcutta, the famous Tagore family established the Bengal School. Here, artists broke away from European styles, and produced new, uniquely Indian modern art, influenced by ancient painting traditions. Nandalal Bose (1883–1966) is the most famous of this group of artists. He painted traditional subjects such as village life and **Hindu** myths using simple folk-art techniques. Many regard him as India's best modern artist.

Modern masters

India's most famous modern artist is Maqbool Fida Husain (born in 1915). He started out painting cinema advertising billboards, but soon gained recognition for his striking, **controversial** artworks. In his oil paintings he uses bold colours and strong brushstrokes, and is a master at showing moods and feelings. Later works include the *Shwetambari* exhibition, which featured sheet-covered walls and hundreds of shredded newspapers. In one public performance he destroyed six of his works by painting over them in white! Husain is also a respected filmmaker.

Painter Amrita Sher-Gil (1913–1941) has a cult following, though she was born in Hungary and died at 28. She is best known for her moody, intense portraits of women, and was strongly influenced by her French art training. Her works have been declared 'National Art Treasures' by the Indian government.

Modern artist M F Husain's **abstract** works are praised around the world.

Textiles

In villages all over India, people still weave cotton or silk cloth, and dye or embroider it to make beautiful textiles. Varanasi is an important centre of silk weaving. *Kinkab* is made there. This **brocade** is woven with gold or silver threads to make **intricate** patterns. A Varanasi *tanchoi sari* is covered with intricate flowers and birds.

Block printing is thought to have been invented in southern India and is still very popular. A piece of wood is carved in raised patterns, then dipped in dye before being stamped on plain cloth. Clothing, bedspreads and tablecloths are commonly made this way for the international market. Another common technique is tie-dyeing. Here, the plain cloth is tightly knotted then dipped into vats of dye. The undyed parts within the knots form swirling, abstract patterns.

Heavenly fabrics

The silk weavers of Varanasi give the patterns of their cloth charming names. An all-over pattern of silver thread is called *mazchar*, meaning 'ripples of silver'. *Chand tara*, woven in gold and silver, means 'moon and stars'.

Tarkashi silver work is made by looping silver wire into delicate patterns.

Metalwork

Some of the world's finest metalwork comes from India. In Orissa, silver is stretched into fine wire and threaded to make delicate filigree work called *tarkashi*. The lace-like effect is used for jewellery, bags and ornamental boxes. This ancient craft dates back more than 1000 years. *Bidri* is a metalwork technique that originated in Iran. Copper and zinc is cast into bowls, urns or plates, then patterns are etched (scratched) into the blackened surface. Silver or gold leaf is then beaten into the grooves to create shining contrasts.

Looking to the future

The rich variety of India's arts and crafts is a reflection of the country's complex and diverse culture. India continues to embrace new ideas as it moves with confidence through the 21st century. It is certain to remain one of the world's most vibrant cultures.

GLOSSARY

abstract   not realistic or not easy to understand

adaptation   re-working; new version

anonymous   by an unknown author

assassinate   murder, usually for political reasons

Bollywood   name for the studios in Mumbai that make many popular Indian movies

brocade   woven fabric with raised pattern

Buddhism   religion in which followers study the teachings of the Buddha and strive for a peaceful state called enlightenment. A follower of Buddhism is a Buddhist.

caste system   ancient Indian system that separates people into higher and lower classes

Christianity   religion based on the belief in one God and the teachings of Jesus, as written in a holy book called the Bible. A follower of Christianity is called a Christian.

civilisation   state in an advanced stage of development

compulsory   required, usually by law

constitution   set of written rules by which a country is governed

controversial   attracting criticism and argument

democracy   form of government in which decisions are made by elected representatives

discriminate   treat people unfairly on the basis of their race, gender or religion, or for some other reason

diverse   various kinds or forms

dowry   money or goods that must be paid to the husband and family of a bride

enlightenment   condition of spiritual peace and understanding

epic   long traditional story about gods and heroes

ethnic group   people who share a specific culture, language and background

fertility   fruitfulness

gesture movement of the body, usually the limbs

Hinduism diverse religion that originated in India; followers worship many gods and goddesses and believe in the rebirth of souls into new bodies after death. A follower of Hinduism is a Hindu.

improvise make up spontaneously

indigenous original or native to a particular country or area

Indus Valley valley of the Indus River, which now flows through Pakistan

intricate finely worked; complicated

Jainism Indian religion founded around 550 BC that teaches detachment from the world and avoiding injury to all living things. A follower is called a Jain.

lentil type of pulse (seed) that is high in protein

life expectancy number of years a person can expect to live

marionette doll-like puppet with movable arms and legs worked by strings from above

migrate move permanently to a new area or country

Mughal Mongolian people from central Asia whose warlike leaders overran northern India and set up an empire there

multicultural made up of several different races and cultures

Muslim having to do with or following Islam, a religion based on belief in one god called Allah. Muslims follow the teachings of the prophet Mohammed, as written in a holy book called the Koran.

partitioned separated into two countries

reincarnation belief that humans are reborn after death

ritual traditional religious or spiritual ceremony

sacred holy or religious

Sanskrit ancient written language of India, distantly related to English

Sikhism religion founded around 500 years ago and based in the Punjab in northern India; it combines aspects of Islam and Hinduism. A follower is called a Sikh.

stupa mound or monument built over the ashes of important people, Buddhist monks or relics

vibrate move rapidly

INDEX

A

Ajanta cave paintings 26
Ambedkar, Dr Bhimrao
    Ramji 9
art 26–28

B

Bangladesh 7
Bhonsle, Asha 19
Bollywood 19, 20, 24, 25
British rule 6
Buddhism 6, 7, 10, 26

C

Calcutta 23, 27, 28
caste system 4, 6, 8, 12, 23
Christianity 7, 10
clothing 13, 14–15

D

Dalits (untouchables)
    6, 7, 8, 9, 12
dance 20–21
Dixit, Madhuri 25
drama 20

E

education 5, 13

F

fashion 15
festivals 10–11
film 24–25
flag 5
folk art 27
food 16–17

G

Gandhi, Mahatma 6, 8, 9
government 4, 6, 8, 9

H

Himalayas 5
Hinduism 4, 6, 7, 8, 9,
    10, 11, 12, 16, 20, 21,
    22, 27, 28
Husain M F 28

I

independence 6, 8
indigenous peoples
    4, 7, 11, 12, 13
Islam 6, 7, 11, 16, 20

J

Jainism 7
jewellery 13, 14, 15

L

languages 4
literature 22–23

M

Mahatma Gandhi 6, 8, 9
marriage 4, 10, 12
metalwork 29
Mughals 6, 16
Mumbai 17, 20, 24
music 18–19
Muslims 6, 7, 11, 16, 20

N

Narayan R K 22
New Delhi 6

P

painting 26–28
Pakistan 6, 7
partition 7
population 4, 5, 7, 9
puppet theatre 21

R

Ramzan (Ramadan) 11
religion 4, 6, 7
religious festivals 10, 11
Roy, Arundhati 23

S

Saigal, Kundan Lal 25
Sanskrit 4, 20, 22
Shankar, Ravi 18
Sikhism 7
Sun temple of Konarak 27

T

Tagore, Rabindranath 23
Taj Mahal 6
television 24–25
textiles 29

V

Varanasi 29
Vedas 7, 8, 22

W

women 8, 9

Books should be returned on or before the
last date stamped below